WHEN THE
WIND BLOWS

WHEN THE WIND BLOWS

by Amy and Richard Hutchings
Photographs by Richard Hutchings

SCHOLASTIC INC.

Cartwheel
·B·O·O·K·S·®

New York Toronto London Auckland Sydney
Mexico City New Delhi Hong Kong Buenos Aires

There is nothing better than old friends. In this case, those old friends are also the editor and art director of this book. This dedication is to our editor, Sonia Black, and our art director, Edie Weinberg. Amy and I wish to thank them for their patience and talent in making the most of our words and photography. Thank you!

—A.H. and R.H.

ISBN 0-439-22355-5

Text copyright © 2002 by Amy and Richard Hutchings.
Illustrations copyright © 2002 by Richard Hutchings.
All rights reserved. Published by Scholastic Inc.
SCHOLASTIC, CARTWHEEL BOOKS, and associated logos
are trademarks and/or registered trademarks of Scholastic Inc.

Library of Congress Cataloging-in-Publication Data available.

12 11 10 9 8 7 6 5 4 3 2 1   02 03 04 05 06

Printed in the U.S.A.
First printing, March 2002

Air is all around us. When air moves we call it wind. Wind can be a mild, gentle breeze. Or it can be a strong, gusty gale. Wind can be a mighty storm or a fierce hurricane.

What happens when the wind blows? Turn the page and see.

Wind makes leaves fall.

We rake fallen leaves into
a great, big pile.

When the wind blows...

leaves scatter everywhere!

When the wind blows, the ocean ripples, waves form . . .

and come crashing to shore.

We hold up umbrellas to protect us from the rain.

When the wind blows...

it turns them inside out!

Wind makes kites fly
high up in the sky.

Wind makes
large sailboats
sail upon the
ocean...

and small sailboats drift across lakes.

When the wind blows, windmills turn.

When the wind blows, a paper airplane flies through the air.

When the wind blows, it tosses your hair.

When the wind blows, flags wave wildly in the breeze.

We collect newspapers to recycle.

We stack them neatly.

When the wind blows…

pages of newspapers

are flung all about!

Pinwheels are fun wind toys.

Whirligigs are fun, too. When the wind blows...

they turn, and spin — faster, faster —
making a terrific, colorful show!

Who knows which way the wind will blow?

The weathervane knows.

Weathervanes point in the direction that the wind blows.